The History
of the
Battle to Save Kelly's Bush
and the Green Ban Movement in the Early 1970s

Margaret Shaw

ISBN 978-0-6453080-1-3
© Copyright Margaret Shaw 1996
First edition June 1996
Originally Published by Buckleys
Curent edition published by Rack and Rune Publishing
rackandrune.com

All rights reserved. No part of this publication may be reproduced or transmitted in any form or by any means without permission.

Margaret Shaw has had an interest in conservation for more than fifty years. In 1966 she was involved in the battle to save the Field of Mars Reserve and became a founding member of the Ryde & Hunter's Hill Flora & Fauna Preservation Society. She lived in Hunters Hill from 1960 to 1984 and was a supporter of the Battlers, and those members of the local community who fought to save Kelly's Bush from development.

As a mature student at The University of Sydney she gained her BA with major in History graduating in 1980. After 22 years as an administrator in the University she completed her MA degree in the Department of History in 1995. Since her retirement she has continued to involve herself in conservation activities.

The thesis for her Masters degree, and subsequent detailed research formed the basis of this book.

Notice prepared for one of the Boll the Billy functions at Kelly's Bush

Acknowledgement

I would like to thank Brian Fletcher, Bicentennial Professor of Australian History at the University of Sydney, for his encouragement during the supervision of this work. A special thanks to my wonderful husband John Shaw for his constant support. My gratitude to Chris Dawson and Trudi Kallir for the loan of the papers and to Chris for our many conversions about Kelly's Bush. To Jack Mundey, Rodney Cavalier, Alice Oppen, Kath Lehany, Sheila Swain and Peter Coleman for their time and for sharing with me their experiences and memories of the Battle to save Kelly's Bush.

My appreciation to Liz Croll for her interest and guidance in preparing this work for publication.

Sadly, In the 25 years since this book was published many of those mentioned above have passed away.

I would like to dedicate this to my dearly departed husband, John Shaw, without who's constant and tireless support this book's publication would not have been possible.

KELLY'S BUSH MUST BE SAVED

It is a symbol and a test case

Widespread support from many Sydney citizens and organizations has encouraged the Battlers to keep battling

A public meeting will be held
at the Hunters Hill Town Hall
on Thursday, 17th June,
commencing at 8.00pm

Authorised by The Battlers for Kelly's Bush
with the support of:

- Australian Wildlife Preservation Society
- Ryde Hunters Hill Flora & Fauna Preservation Society
- Australian Labor Party (Hunters Hill Branch)
- Lane Cove Bushland Preservation Society
- Australia Party (Hunters Hill Branch)
- Save the Lane Cove Valley Committee
- C.R.A.G.
- Hunters Hill Trust
- Villa Maria Youth Group

**BREAK ALL OTHER ENGAGEMENTS
IF YOU CARE YOU MUST COME**

Notice of Meeting at which public support was demonstrated for first Green Ban, 17 June 1971

Contents

Introduction	1
Ryde - Hunter's Hill	7
Kelly's Bush - Early History	11
Hunter's Hill Trust	15
The Battlers Formed	19
A Crisis for the Battlers	29
Unions in the First Green Ban	35
A Green Ban at the Rocks	45
Other Important Green Bans	53
A Split in the BLF	55
Victory for the Battlers	57
Conclusion	61
Bibliography	65

Introduction

The 1950s will be remembered by historians as a time of growth and economic recovery for Australia and for those nations devastated by World War II. Britain and Europe and the defeated Germany and Japan set about rebuilding their devastated cities with help from America's Marshall Plan. Both in Australia and overseas, factories that had been producing war machinery now turned to peacetime production. Cars, washing machines and refrigerators rolled off the production line as nations' economies boomed and by the end of the decade Japan and Germany were praised as economic miracles.

Australians in the 1950s were now able to purchase their first Holden car and other major consumer items not available during wartime. There was full employment, a growing population and the arrival of large numbers of migrants willing to work in the new expanding secondary industries. During this stable period most people were preoccupied with family and material comfort, content with the stability of the conservative Menzies Government.

One of the most important tasks facing the Government of the 1950s was to address the problem of inadequate housing.

It is hard to imagine today just how difficult it was to rent or buy a house in Sydney in the early 1950s, due to the ban on home building during World War II and the large increase in population.

The Cumberland County Council had been established, in 1947, in an attempt by the State Government to coordinate planning for the metropolitan area, to keep a balance between development and open space, as they tried to overcome the post-war housing shortage. Although it survived until 1963, its directions were often ignored leaving decisions in the hands of the developers.

At this time many saw environmental issues as hindering development. On the outskirts of Sydney, the State Housing Commission created whole new suburbs, often needlessly removing the trees. The result of this attitude was the sprawling of Sydney as suburbs grew up without provision of services. There was little to recommend much of the housing constructed during this period, except that it offered a roof over the head. Bolton explains[1], 'The suburbs spread like squeezed tooth paste. The local authorities abandoned any pretence of providing bitumen roads before subdivision. Instead, home builders in the new suburbs had to wait several years before the coming of made roads and guttering, and then these were provided at the expense of the householders.'

In the inner suburbs old but often beautiful homes were demolished and replaced by cramped blocks of units without thought to the environment or the wishes of nearby residents or those who would inhabit them. As Lloyd describes[2], 'The residue of the past was swept away by a tide of modern enterprise, conditioned by beliefs that Australia's natural environment was infinite, and that as a young country its man-made fabric was not worth preserving.'

Eventually dissatisfaction with this unrestrained growth, and the environmental problems that these piecemeal decisions caused, would be one of the factors contributing to the climate of unrest as the 1960s progressed.

During the last years of the Menzies era Australia was seen by other countries as a safe haven for investment. This factor together with the exploitation of new minerals, previously unknown in Australia, brought many new investors with their capital into Australia, as companies grew up overnight and fortunes were made and lost on the stock exchange. America was a particularly keen investor as Bolton describes[3], 'In 1964, 20 per cent of Australian manufacturing had American ownership, in 1965, 27 per cent.'

Nowhere was affluence more apparent than in the city of Sydney where the flood of overseas capital contributed to the building boom of the middle to late 1960s. Flower describes[4], 'The scale of the city began to change dramatically as prestige office blocks began to shoot skywards in the main business area. Well known (and often well loved) landmarks disappeared almost overnight to be replaced by yawning chasms of sandstone awaiting the latest in bland glass slabs of curtain walling.'

After twenty years of postwar boom a small number of developers had made fortunes. However, much of the growth was in the private sector and while it had been encouraged by State Governments, particularly in New South Wales they had at the same time often neglected the provision of adequate public facilities, ·such as sewerage, decent roads and urban transport. All too often growth took place without regard to the effect it would have on the environment. By the late 1960s some Australians were questioning this growth and were becoming increasingly concerned about so called "progress" that took no account of environmental concerns. Evidence of this can be seen with the establishment in 1965 of The Australian Conservation Foundation, it was important because it gave a respectability to the environmental movement, being outside party politics it played an early role in mobilising public opinion on environmental matters.

The political scene in New South Wales during this postwar period had been dominated by the Labor Party led by Bob Heffernan. Although he stepped down before the 1965 election, in favour of Jack Renshaw, it was not hard for Robert Askin, to portray the Labor Party as out of touch, living in the past and failing to appeal to the young, with an average age of Cabinet members at 61. Prior to the election the Government struggled unsuccessfully to come to terms within its own ranks on issues such as State Aid to Catholic Schools and the sensitive issue of shopping hours. During the 1965 campaign it alienated teachers, railwaymen, and public servants by the clumsy handling of a pay claim. As Turner describes[5], 'Labor became vulnerable mainly because of its complacent and insensitive administration and insufficient attention to the political costs of its actions. Under Askin, the Opposition became more credible'

The elections of May 1965 were very close. The Liberal Party was able to pick up enough votes to win with the support of those disaffected by Labor and also with some of the Catholic vote. Askin had led the Liberal Party out of 24 years in the wilderness and would present a new formidable political force in New South Wales. Hickie describes the situation at the time[6]; 'Almost single-handed he had rescued his party from its long years as a parliamentary punching-bag for overwhelming Labor majorities and had turned it into a working organisation ... Askin changed the Liberal Party into one which commanded wide popular respect.' He was a clever, pragmatic politician, who cared little about policy and he would find no problems with the big developers as they began increasingly to call the tune in the city of Sydney and the suburbs. As Mundey explains[7], 'Sir Robert Askin slavishly followed the whims and wishes of the property developers. Construction was for profit not for use'. As the victory of Askin in New South Wales marked the beginnings of a shift in traditional political values and allegiances, so it was Australia's involvement in the Vietnam war and its response to the growing protest movements overseas that became the chief catalyst for change leading to the participation of ordinary people in political affairs in much of Australia.

In the United States, works such as Rachel Carson's. "The Silent Spring" shocked many Americans as it described the pollution being caused by industrial technology, while Paul Ehrlich's studies challenged traditional views on population growth. Also, at this time, the black American population began their civil rights movement. In France, in May 1968, students and workers brought Paris to a standstill with riots and strikes as they protested at the handling of the economy and the way the Universities were being organised. Somehow, in the late 1960s, the world stirred as never before in recent memory. No doubt the media played a role, when the Vietnam war and other disturbing world events came daily into our lounge rooms. As the anti-Vietnam-War movement gathered momentum, it provided a focus for other groups fighting for a better deal, such as our Aboriginal population, the Women's Movement and the newly formed Resident Action Groups. People from many different economic backgrounds who had never been involved in protest movements now wanted to make their voices heard. This awareness produced a new political consciousness from which the environmental movement would grow.

1. Geoffrey Bolton, Spoils and Spoilers, Allen & Unwin, Sydney, 1981, 153.
2. Geoffrey Bolton, (Quoting C Lloyd, the National Estate: Australia's Heritage, Stanmore 1977 p 11)
3. 3 Geoffrey Bolton, The Oxford History of Australia, Vol. 5 The Middle Way 1942-1988, OUP, Melbourne 1990,92.
4. Cedric Flower, Illustrated History of New South Wales, Rigby Publishers, Sydney, 207.
5. J. Hagen & K. Turner, A History of the Labor Party in New South Wales 1891-1991, Longman Cheshire, Melbourne, 1991,193.
6. 6 David Hickie, The Prince and the Premier, Angus & Robertson, Sydney, 1985, 52.
7. Jack Mundey, Preventing the Plunder, in V.Burgman & J.Lee Eds, Staining the Wattle, McPhee Gribble/Penguin, Victoria, 1988, 175

Ryde - Hunter's Hill

During 1966 in the Ryde/Gladesville area I became closely involved in one of the first groups of resident action in Sydney. Their aim was to save "The Field of Mars Reserve" from being used as a garbage tip. The area involved was 100 acres of Crown land originally proclaimed as a reserve for public recreation in 1887. It consisted of two creeks and, being heavily wooded, was a haven for birds and native flora and fauna. It also contained examples of subtropical rainforest, together with wet and dry sclerophyll forest. The Reserve was regularly used by local residents and for nature expeditions by the local Schools. However, Ryde Council at this time, in order to dispose of an increasing amount of garbage, turned their attention to the Field of Mars. The Council in 1966 was dominated by a group of very conservative Labor aldermen who represented all the worst aspects of environmental thinking of the 1950s and 1960s. In some cases they had a professional interest in Real Estate and were more interested in disposing of the Municipality's waste than in preserving bushland. They were not aware of the new growing concern in the local community about environmental pollution and the need to preserve bushland for its own sake. To these aldermen the Field of Mars was just an open space to be filled in with garbage while the remaining area would be useful for home sites.

Many of the residents were, like myself, parents from the local schools whose children had grown up to enjoy the bush. In 1966 these residents decided to form the Ryde & Hunter's Hill Flora and Fauna Preservation Society (RHHFFPS). I was one of the founding members and it was from this commitment that my interest in the local environment grew and led to my further involvement in the Battle for Kelly's Bush. The Society's aim was to prevent not only the current threat of a tip, but to ensure that the Reserve remain as refuge in a suburban area for our native flora and fauna, with its status unquestioned in the years to come. The Society worked to alert local organisations and· Ryde Council of its great value to the community. At the next local government elections it successfully supported the candidacy of those who, as aldermen, would be sympathetic to retaining the Reserve in its natural state. As a result of these efforts the Council agreed to abandon its plans for a tip and has worked ever since with the .RHHFFPS to maintain the Reserve as a Wildlife Refuge. In 1987, a Field Studies Centre was erected to enable School children from all over Sydney to study the variety of flora and fauna the reserve has to offer. The success of this early urban resident action, as with the Battle to save Kelly's Bush, was due to the dedication and persistence of a small group of people. Perhaps the most remarkable of these was the late Rod Wallace who joined the Society as a junior member at age 12 and at the time of his death in 1988, aged 35, was in his ninth year as President. His entire life was devoted to environmentalism and to the preservation of the Field of Mars. The growing awareness of the environment during the 1970s and 1980s owes much to the dedication of such people. Speaking at his Memorial service in the Field of Mars Reserve, Rodney Cavalier, previously the Local Member, paid this tribute[1] ; 'He was able to see beyond this narrow stretch of urban bush - as magnificent as it is. He perceived that there were greater truths involved here. It was not just a matter of the urban sprawl of Sydney or the land mass of NSW and Australia ... Rod saw that this was a cause as wide as the planet.'

Peter Coleman, the local state Member of Parliament at the time, remarked that the preservation of the Field of Mars Reserve was an important victory so early in the conservation movement and he knew that it meant a great deal to many local residents. He agreed that, outside the municipalities of Ryde and Hunter's Hill, little was known of the efforts of those residents involved in this campaign.

When, shortly afterwards, the battle to save Kelly's Bush commenced in the neighbouring Municipality of Hunter's Hill, much that had been learned in the struggle to save the Field of Mars was found to be helpful.

However, none of us would have forseen the amount of media-attention that this struggle would receive, both in Australia and overseas, by attracting the world's first Green Ban.

The history of the first Green Ban in Australia is made all the more interesting in that it occurred in the peaceful upper middle-class suburbs of Hunter's Hill and Woolwich. The Municipality of Hunter's Hill, the oldest in Australia, was proclaimed in 1861 by the Governor, Sir William Denison. Many of the beautiful buildings, still standing, were designed by two young French brothers Didier and Jules Joubert. Unlike so many municipalities whose existence depends upon a line drawn on a map, its situation on a peninsular, bounded by the Parramatta and Lane Cove rivers, added to its charm and sense of seclusion. An article in the Daily Mirror newspaper of April 1961 describes 'The leafy streets and old garden walls, houses of warm, honey coloured stone from simple cottages to imposing mansions, form a picture quite unusual in Australia. A century ago, before bridges and regular ferries ended its isolation, this was the "French Village" and there is still something faintly exotic about the atmosphere of Hunter's Hill.'

To many residents of Hunter's Hill, in spite of regular bus and ferry services of the 1960s, there was still a sense of being a separate and unique part of Sydney. The peninsular was traditionally conservative and represented by conservative politicians and aldermen. However, by the middle 1960s many residents were becoming concerned about retaining its character and, by the end of the 1960s, were alarmed at the rapid unit development and the demolition of many old stone houses in the name of progress. Now, in retrospect, it is interesting that it was to be the battle to save a piece of bushland rather than the preservation of its historic buildings .that would be the focus of so much interest and controversy in the late 1960s and early 1970s.

---

1. R Cavalier, Speech at the Memorial Service for Rod Wallace, Field of Mars Reserve, Friday 16 December 1988.
2. Geoffrey Scott, Sunday Mirror, April 18, 1965

Aboriginal pond in Kelly's Bush

Kelly's Bush - Early History

Kelly's Bush is a unique piece of bushland situated in the municipality of Hunter's Hill in the suburb of Woolwich on the Sydney Harbour foreshores of the Parramatta River. The reason that this area is unique is that it remains the last piece of natural bushland visible on the western reaches of the Sydney Harbour foreshores. In one of the many letters about this subject written to the Sydney Morning Herald (9/10/1970) R.N. Walker, Director of the National Trust of Australia (NSW), explains[1], 'Local communities, striving desperately to save their "bit of bush", tend to seek expert scientific pronouncements on its special, unique features. This should not be necessary – the true value is simply that it is a quite ORDINARY bit of natural bush. Its uniqueness lies in the fact that it has miraculously survived and continues to exist so near the city and still warrants the evocative and intriguing name of Kelly's Bush.' In the late 1960s through the mid 1970s this stretch of bushland would become the centre of one of the most interesting and controversial struggles in Green Politics in Australia. It would involve the Hunter's Hill Council, the National Trust, the Hunter's Hill Trust, both the ruling State Liberal Party and the Labor Party Opposition, the State Planning Authority and last, but most importantly, the local residents and Unions.

Eventually the bushland would be saved from development only by the unusual alliance of a group of middleclass women known as the "Battlers for Kelly's Bush" and the Secretary of the NSW Builders Labourers Federation, Jack Mundey, who with other unions applied the world's first Green Ban. Kelly's Bush derived its name from T H Kelly who, in 1892, established a smelting works on 2 acres of the land leaving the remaining 17 acres as a buffer between his industry and the local residents of Hunter's Hill. This was an unusual industrial development for a largely residential area and demonstrates the early use of buffer zones between incompatible land uses. The area remained unchanged until 1956 when the Hunter's Hill Council, desiring to obtain parkland for the residents and together with the Cumberland County Council, purchased seven acres of the "Open Space" area. Known as Weil Park, the area was developed into a grassed oval to provide for various sporting activities.

In 1963 the Cumberland County Council was replaced by the State Planning Authority (SPA) which was approached in 1966 by the Town Clerk, at the direction of Hunter's Hill Council, to secure more of the Open Space land. Quoting from the Council correspondence[2], 'the Council feels it is important to the interest of posterity that additional "open space" area should be acquired whilst the opportunity exists'.

In June 1967 the Smelting Works were no longer viable on the Hunter's Hill site and the company moved to Alexandria. Also, at this time, the firm of AV Jennings took a two-year option to buy the land and, in submitting a development plan for high-rise housing on the site, applied to Council for the suspension of the original zoning. An extract from Council minutes of 24 June illustrates the council's opposition to the development.[3] 'Council is unanimously and emphatically opposed to any alteration in the zoning of the part of land at Woolwich owned by the Sydney Smelting Co Pty Ltd, which has been zoned under the County of Cumberland Planning Scheme as "Open Space" since 1951.' Council also renewed its appeal to the State Planning Authority for acquisition of the land. However in July of that year the final reply came from the State Planning Authority that it could not afford to purchase the land for "Open Space".

1. R.N. Walker, Director National Trust of Australia, (NSW) Sydney Morning Herald, September 10, 1970.
2. Hunter's Hill Council Minutes, 1966
3. Hunter's Hill Council Minutes, 24 June 1968.

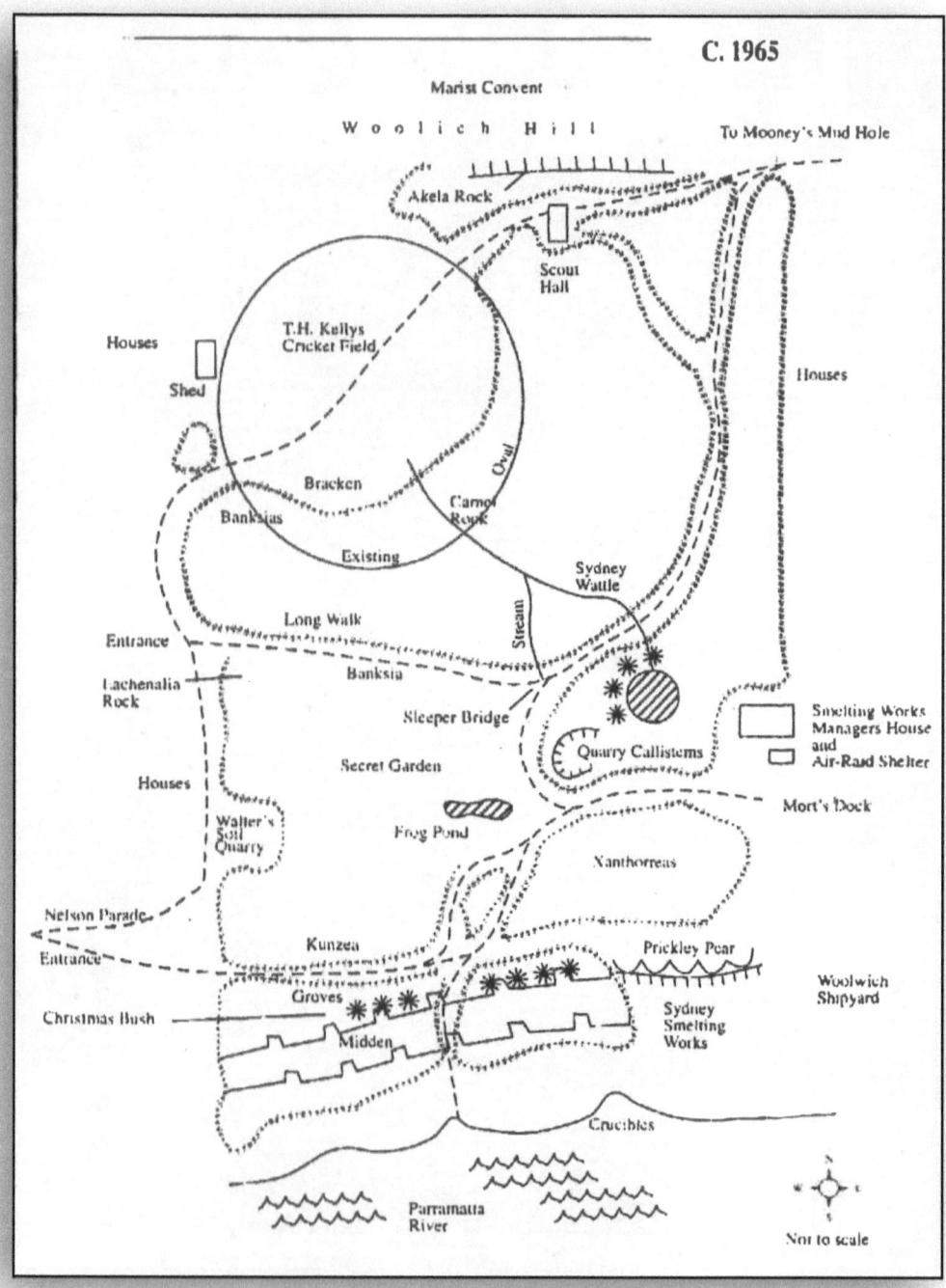

Personal "Mud Map" of Kelly's Bush by Michael Lehany, Battle Kath Lehany's son who during his childhood looked on Kelly's Bush as his playground

Hunter's Hill Trust

At the same time there occurred another event that made Hunter's Hill residents more aware of their local environment. In 1968 a group of local residents, quite disturbed at the loss of several famous historic homes and the lack of recognition of the history of the Municipality by some aldermen, called a meeting in the Town Hall. The meeting was one of the largest ever held in the Municipality and on 7 February 1968 the Hunter's Hill Trust was formed. Their task was to keep the unique charact.er of Hunter's Hill and to work for the selection of aldermen who supported their objectives . They enjoyed a high profile in the local community and there is no doubt that the Trust raised the consciousness of the many local residents who regularly attended the meetings. It was not surprising, therefore, that the first proposal for high-density housing on Kelly's Bush was rejected unanimously by the Council.

The Hunter's Hill Trust put a great effort into selecting sympathetic candidates for the next Council election by supporting only those who pledged to pursue its aims. The election was held at the end of 1968 and all those candidates, supported by the Trust, were elected. To those residents dedicated to the preservation of Kelly's Bush it seemed that the battle was over.

However, this was not the situation as Roddewig describes,[1] 'The real battle had not yet started. Though Kelly's Bush was just one among many issues in the election, it seemed that the victory of the trust candidates would guarantee its preservation. That was not to be. AV Jennings began to alter plans and to line up support among State Government friends, including the Chairman of the New South Wales State Planning Authority.'

Then a new proposal was put forward: the State Planning Authority, on behalf of the Government, would purchase 5.6 acres of waterfront land at Kelly's Bush, for public use, at a cost of $176,000. Because this land was not suitable for building purposes, this proposal would be of advantage to Jennings as he could retain the remaining 6.5 acres to put forward a more acceptable development to the Council. It was also becoming obvious at this stage that some aldermen, in spite of their pledge to support Trust policy, were not opposed to some development of Kelly's Bush. They believed that this new initiative by the SPA to preserve the foreshore area of the bush would placate their opposition.

This was not the case as the debate in Council and in the local community was still very bitter. Firstly there was strong criticism of the fact that the area proposed for public recreation was steeply sloping foreshore land, of little use as a public reserve, as this part of the bush was not used by the local residents. The Trust constantly reminded the aldermen of their pledge to support Trust policy with no success. Then as Council records explain [2], 'A series of modified applications were subsequently submitted by the Jennings Group and disapproved, before Council, in November 1969, agreed in principle that it would favour suspension of the zoning to enable a strictly controlled town-house type of development.' The Council was sharply divided with the voting 5 to 4 in favour of suspending the Open Space zoning. Alderman Coombes, a keen supporter of the Trust, gave verbal notice of his intention to move a rescission motion at the next Meeting. He had no political affiliations, however, unlike some of his fellow alderman recently elected on the Trust ticket, he was still firmly opposed to development and very angry at the betrayal of those now voting in favour. However, the motion was lost on the same lines as the original one in favour of development.

The Hunter's Hill Trust wrote to the Council stating that the land should be acquired as a public reserve. It also held two Public meetings with the majority of members claiming[3] , 'Council should not acquiesce to the Jennings proposal'. There were many in the Trust who now felt that their battle to save the Bush was futile. However, their efforts had reduced the size of the development to 25 suburban houses and when Pat Morton, the Minister for Local Government, later visited the site he agreed that 25 single dwellings was the maximum number he would permit. As the debate continued in the local Council and community there was still a strong feeling among some residents that any development, no matter how small, should not be permitted. They believed this area of bush belonged to all and to sacrifice it for the sake of twenty-five homes was wrong.

This point of view is expressed by Walker, Director of the National Trust[4], 'Apart from all other values such lands must be recognised also as air-pollution controls, for their function in giving us clean air and a city in which people· can breathe safely. All of this, tangible and intangible, is threatened by the intrusion of a patch of twenty-five-house suburbia···. A drop in the housing ocean - as against so much for so many!'

1. R.J. Roddewig, Green Bans, Hale & Ironmonger, Sydney, 1978, 5
2. Hunters Hill Council Minutes, 10 November, 1969
3. Hunters Hill Trust Meeting 10 November, 1969
4. R.N. Walker, Director, National Trust of Australia (NSW) Sydney Morning Herald. 10 September, 1970.

Photograph from a pamphlet entitled "The Truth About Kelly's Bush"
published by Hunter's Hill Trust

The Battlers Formed

As concern about the proposed development grew some local residents felt there was a need for a new group, separate from the Trust, to fight solely for the preservation of the bush. Thirteen local women, some housewives who had lived in the area for many years and whose children had grown up with Kelly's Bush as their playground, banded together to fight for the preservation of all of Kelly's Bush. The Battlers for Kelly's Bush was formed at a well attended meeting in the All-Saints Parish Hall on 27 September, 1970.

From the beginning it was obvious that this group of well educated, determined women would leave no stone unturned in this difficult task. Kath Lehaney, Secretary of the Battlers, in a retrospective article in April 1991, explains[1], 'We were from all sides of the political spectrum, people who were religious, non-religious, people who had lived here forever and relative newcomers.' Their first letter to the local newspaper, the Weekly Times, describes the sentiments of the group[2], 'It is remarkable to have twelve acres of "bush" so close to the heart of Sydney; it contains aboriginal rock engravings and a pool; it is the nesting place of numerous bush birds and it is a living museum for natural-science students in botany, geology, archaeology and environmental study. It is also an area where families may walk and enjoy bush and harbour views; it is an ordinary piece of bushland where today's youth can play as we did when young ... Once this land is taken, it can never be returned. It will be useless saying, in twenty years time, -"we should have kept this land, let's bulldoze down the houses"- it will be too late.'

As the debate in the local community continued the Battlers for Kelly's Bush lost no time before beginning a letter-writing campaign and arranging interviews with all local aldermen, followed by deputations to Peter Coleman, the local Liberal member of State Parliament, and to the Premier Robert Askin. They made a direct appeal to the Hunters Hill Council supported by documents and a petition by local residents. They petitioned the State Planning Authority, the proposed developers, AV Jennings, and the Leader of the Opposition, Pat Hills. Monica Sheehan, one of the most active of the Battlers, describes[3]; 'With almost apostolic zeal, we contacted alderman, politicians, friends, shopkeepers, writers, environmentalists etc., and wrote numerous articles for the press; hundreds of small card-letters were distributed for friends to send to the Premier, and various functions, aimed at publicising and seeking assistance for our cause, were held.'

The Battlers were successful from the beginning in gaining some media attention both in the local press and in the Sydney daily papers. Four of the Battlers were photographed in the Sydney Morning Herald of 22 October 1970 with an article entitled "Mums, dads and kids, fighting for a bit of countryside in the heart of the city". This article also reported that[4], 'Pat Hills, Leader of the State Opposition, promised a Labor Government would resume the land if successful at the next state elections. It also reported that Peter Coleman, MLA for Fuller, would introduce a deputation of Battlers to Pat Morton but points out that the Government has limited finance.' The Battlers then set about raising money to assist the Government to buy the bush as the lack of public money to acquire the land was one of the arguments presented by those who were pushing for its development.

To show residents the bush before it was destroyed the Battlers held what they referred to as Boil-the-Billy functions which were attended by people from many parts of Sydney.

These proved very successful and gained coverage in the media. The aim was to demonstrate what a tragedy it would be to lose the bush for the erection of just twenty-five suburban homes -the motto of the Battlers was becoming 'Kelly's Bush Now What Next'.

The next move for the Battlers was a meeting with Premier Askin, with the Local member, Peter Coleman, in attendance. He went on to explain[5], 'the Premier felt he had to meet the Battlers as already they had attracted some media attention, and controversy in the electorate'.

On Tuesday 27 October, 1970 a deputation of nine members of the Battlers for Kelly's Bush Committee requested[6], 'that the Premier intervene and stop the suspension of the County Scheme on the 6.5 remaining acres of land ... and declare that the alienation of the area by housing development will not be permitted ... This Deputation most earnestly believes that this land must be preserved for posterity ... that so little natural bushland left around the foreshores of the Sydney Harbour, it is a crime against our children to destroy it'. Therefore 'this deputation realizes that the Government may be required to purchase the land if the "reserve open space" zoning is retained' ... so ... ·asks the Premier to accept the assistance of the Battlers for Kelly's Bush Fund to provide some of the purchase price.'

Chris Dawson, one of the executive members of the Battlers, reports of the meeting[7], 'Robert Askin's response to their petition was very polite although his manner was a little paternal. However, he appeared impressed with the way we had presented our case and suggested to Peter Coleman that it might be a good idea to "FREEZE" any re-zoning until more time could be given to the matter. We were very happy at this suggestion. However, Coleman then stated to the Premier that there might be another block of land which local residents might want to be purchased in the future, i.e., Clarke's Point. The Premier then withdrew his suggestion much to the disappointment of the Battlers.'

Peter Coleman had given a lot of his time listening to the case for saving Kelly's Bush and he had a good reputation and was a keen conscientious local Member. In this professional role he also understood and represented the point of view of those who, like Mayor Farrant (Mayor of Hunter's Hill), favoured development. It was now obvious to the Battlers that he, as with some of the Council aldermen, favoured development of Kelly's Bush because they preferred that any land to be acquired by the Government should be at Clarke's Point. Coleman explained that he felt[8], 'a reserve at

Clarke's Point would be a great asset to the local community, something that children and people could enjoy not just in ten but one hundred years from now'. He went on to explain that, 'in spite of the sympathetic hearing the Premier gave to the Battlers, Askin was not a man with an eye· to the needs of future generations or to the need to preserve open space for its own sake. His idea of green would be the traditional park at the end of the street. He was of the generation of politicians who prized development above all else and he could never see beyond the next election.'

Unfortunately, the situation at Clarke's Point on the Woolwich peninsula would continue to confuse the Battle for Kelly's Bush. A brochure entitled "The Truth about Kelly's Bush", produced, at the time, for the Hunter's Hill Trust Committee, explains[9], 'The case for saving Kelly's Bush has been prejudiced in some people's minds by the need to keep industry off Clarke's Point, and the apparent impossibility of achieving both.' This area comprising 8 acres, was originally part of the industrial holding of the Morts Dock and Engineering Company and was used in conjunction with Woolwich Graving Dock. The significance of Clarke's Point was that it formed the western focal point of Sydney Harbour. However, it would require significant rehabilitation to make it viable as a public reserve. Monica Sheehan of the Battlers explains [10], 'Apparently research into deep-water facilities was being carried out by Baral and aldermen living in this vicinity (Clarke's Point) were apprehensive that industry might operate near their backyards. Therefore, they decided to approach Council or Government to acquire it as a reserve.' This argument is strengthened by Battler Kath Lehany who, as quoted by Roddewig, attributed the change in Council's vote at the end of 1969 to the Clarke's Point situation[11], 'There were lots of rumours about why the council changed its mind, the one we gave most weight to said the Minister for Local Government had informed the council that it would not stop any further light-industrial development at Clarke's Point, unless the Council approved the Jennings/SPA proposal. The Council did not want any new industry in their quiet residential enclave.' In retrospect it would appear that this interpretation of Council's attitude by the Battlers was correct.

In a short history of Kelly's Bush available from Hunter's Hill Council 'the elimination of waterfront industry' was given as one of the provisions in the negotiations with the State Planning Authority on June 1971.

The Battlers continued to try and influence public opinion about the value of keeping the Bush and sought help and advice from many organisations. They wrote to Prince Phillip and Sir Garfield Barwick and although their letters were politely acknowledged no help was forthcoming. As described in Honi Soit, June 17 1973, 'they also sought the support and cooperation from groups in Hunter's Hill and the conservation Trusts and Societies throughout the suburbs of Sydney, plus the Australia wide associations, including the National Trust, National Parks & Wildlife Service and the Australian Conservation Foundation.' Records from the Mitchell Library also reveal support from the Royal Australian Institute of Architects, (NSW Chapter), the Civic Design Society (University of NSW) and the Royal Botanical Gardens.

The next move in the Battle for Kelly's Bush was a Public meeting supported by the Hunter's Hill and National Trusts held on 5 November 1970 in the All-Saints Church Hall, Hunter's Hill. Battler Chris Dawson describes the meeting as being successful and praises the excellent address delivered by Mary Campbell of the National Trust. Mrs Campbell, speaking of the role of women, describes[14], 'the particular force that women have is -their persistence against all odds, their bland ignoring of all side issues- a singleness of purpose that won't be deflected and which takes them sailing serenely into the sacred halls of power. She went on 'Our practical realist says, "we must have balance, the trouble with the bush cranks is they won't accept a compromise - carve the disputed bush down the middle - half to development, half to the bush boys"'. But the time for this sort of balance is long gone the proper balance now is to save all the remaining bushland as against all that has gone. Reflecting on this address it is interesting that it would be the "persistence" of the Battlers that would sustain them over the years when they would often be seen as "bush cranks" by many in their local community.

On 18 November the Battlers visited Coleman at Parliament house, hoping to apply some political pressure in view of the forthcoming State election. The seat of Fuller was not a particularly safe one for the Government and Coleman's Labor opponent was a well known barrister Tony Bellanto. He gave them a good hearing and stated that 'Kelly's Bush subdivision will not be carried out until plans for the area are reviewed'.

In spite of this assurance and the efforts of the Battlers and others who had written and petitioned the Council, Premier, and Minister for Local Government, the Council on 24 November 1970 agreed to suspend the zoning on Kelly's Bush from Reserve Open Space and recommend that it be rezoned Recommended for Residential Development. Then on 2 December at a meeting of the General Purposes Committee to consider Town Planning matters the "Kelly's Bush" proposed development was discussed in detail and it seemed now that all that was needed for the project to go ahead was that Jennings finalise their plans and that the Minister for Local Government agree to the change of zoning.

The Battlers met again with Coleman on 19 December and endeavoured once more to persuade him of the regional significance of Kelly's Bush, claiming it was not just a local matter. In a letter dated 23 December 1970 they set out to clarify the points that he had made at the meeting and to give their comments on them. The letter concludes[15], 'We wish to point out that the inevitable consequence of a Government policy which leaves the final say on such matters as "Kelly's Bush" to local Councils would, in the end, lead to the disappearance of most open space. Sooner or later local and other pressures build up to use the space for housing, bowling clubs or other restricted purposes. Each loss is a permanent and irreversible one.'

Council records of the period from 5 October 1969 to December 1970 contain many letters from individual residents about the subject of Kelly's Bush. Although the majority were opposed to development, there were some residents strongly in favour of the Jennings proposal. The main reasons given were the chance to expedite the provision of sewerage to the areas where it was needed, the proposal that the State Planning Authority would acquire the waterfront land at no cost to Council and the fear that, if no development were to take place, Council would be forced to steeply increase rates to pay for acquisition of the rest of Kelly's Bush. It is possible to gauge through these records ·some measure of the controversy that existed in the local community at this time as arguments for and against development were debated at Council, local meetings and in the local press.

Kath Lehaney explains how[16], 'Mayor Farrant, who strongly favoured development, felt so threatened by the Battlers, that he decided to have them investigated. However, there was nothing to be revealed and he eventually realised that they were an ordinary group of housewives who were determined to save a dozen acres of bushland. It was one of our great strengths that we had no personal or financial gain except to see the bush retained as open space for all to enjoy.'

The year 1971 started with the State election campaign in full swing and with the Leader of the Opposition, Pat Hills, stating[17], 'that when Labor is returned at the next election the land will be acquired and reserved for public use for all time. If necessary, amending legislation will be passed to preserve this valuable piece of foreshore land'. Tony Bellanto, the Labor candidate, campaigned strongly on the Kelly's Bush issue, however, there was no word from Premier Askin although the Battlers pressed him for an answer. Then just two days before the election they received a telegram that raised their hopes. 'RE YOUR TELEGRAM STOP VERY HOPEFUL OF A HELPFUL DECISION ON YOUR PROBLEMS AND WILL ADVISE WITHIN 24 HOURS R W ASKIN PREMIER.' This was a last minute bid by Askin who was becoming increasingly anxious about the seat of Fuller which, if it went to the Opposition, could mean the loss of Government. Time went by and there was no further word from the Premier, as the Government was returned and Peter Coleman was re-elected.

As Hardman explains[18], 'All further correspondence, somewhat naive jogs to the memory of the Premier about the telegram he had sent, were answered with the routine reply: " ... and the matter is being investigated". This was a difficult time for the Battlers.

Kath Lehaney, the Secretary, explains[19], 'it was now becoming difficult to keep up the momentum in the struggle to save the "Bush". Although the Hunter's Hill Trust could still muster a majority vote to continue fighting for preservation of the bushland, with the threat of high-rise removed, the community in general lost interest. Many people seemed to feel that we should not stop other people from being able to enjoy the benefits of living in Hunter's Hill as long as the homes fit the neighbourhood'.

1. Sydney Morning Herald, 8 April 1991.
2. The Weekly Times, 7 October 1970.
3. Monica Sheehan Battlers for Kelly's Bush, ML MSS 5549/box 3
4. Tony Stephens, Sydney Morning Herald, 22 October 1970
5. Interview with Peter Coleman, 10 October 1995.
6. Macquarie University Students Journal Arena, September 1971.
7. Interview with Battler Chris Dawson, 5 October 1995.
8. Interview with Peter Coleman, 10 October 1995.
9. Hunters Hill Trust Pamphlet on behalf of Dr A Bradfield and Committee Members, Undated.
10. Monica Sheehan Battlers for Kellys Bush, ML MSS 5549/box 3.
11. Richard Roddewig, Green Bans, Hale Ironmonger, Sydney, 1978 6
12. Monica Sheehan Battlers for Kelly's Bu·sh, ML.MSS.5549/box 3
13. The Battle for Kelly's Bush, Honi Soit, 17 June 1971
14. Mary Campbell, Address to Public Meeting, 5 November 1970
15. Kath Lehany on Behalf of Battlers, Letter to Peter Coleman, 23 December 1970
16. Battler Kath Lehany, Interview, 19 October 1995
17. Honi Soit, op. cit.
18. M. Hardman & P. Manning. Green Bans, Australian Conservation, Melbourne, 1975.
19. R.J. Roddewig, op. cit, 7.

BACK TO KELLY'S BUSH

KELLY'S BUSH IS ABOUT TO BE LOST
DESPITE THE ENVIRONMENT COST
BUT IF YOU JOIN OUR PUSH
WE'LL SHOW THAT THE BUSH
IS WORTH MORE THAN A LUXURY BLOCK

SUNDAY AUGUST 8
COMMENCING AT 11:00 A.M.

BRING : FAMILY AND FRIENDS
       : FOOD AND DRINK
BABECUE AND BOIL A BILLY

ORGANISED BY NEWLY FORMED 'KELLY'S BUSH CITIZENS ACTION' COMMITTEE
IN SUPPORT OF THE 'BATTLE FOR KELLY'S BUSH'.

BREAK ALL OTHER ENGAGEMENTS
IF YOU CARE YOU MUST COME

A Crisis for the Battlers

One group in the local community was becoming more interested in the Kelly's Bush issue, the Hunter's Hill Branch of the Australian Labor Party. At the annual Branch elections in March 1971 an elderly conservative executive was replaced by an entirely new group of enthusiastic young people committed to community'involvement and, in particular, the preservation of Kelly's Bush. The most important of the group in this context was the newly elected President, Rodney Cavalier, who would become Local Member in 1978 and Minister for Education in the Wran Government. At this point in his career, Cavalier was an official with the Miscellaneous Workers Union. Soon after his election as President he contacted the Battlers and invited them to meet with him to discuss tactics in the battle to save the "Bush". Cavalier describes how[1], 'the more conservative members of the group were very suspicious of him, a member of the Left of the ALP, with Union involvement.' However, he was impressed with their dedication and the effort they had already made to save the Bush. He went on to relate how it took several meetings before they were convinced that he was a true conservationist and that they could work together. He then described how he had explained the role the Trade Unions could play if all else failed and said that he would be prepared to help present the case to them if this was necessary.

The situation deteriorated further when, on the 24 May 1971, Hunter's Hill Council signed an agreement giving approval to the development of Kelly's Bush. Monica Sheehan describes the next event[2], 'At the end of May the Premier contacted the President, Betty James stating, "you will need to pull a rabbit out of a hat" to save the Bush, because Mr Morton will sign the re-zoning document in the next few days.' The Battlers immediately sent telegrams to Askin, Morton and Sir Albert Jennings protesting. Chris

Dawson recalls Askin's attitude as he responded[3], 'I can't prevent Mr Morton from signing the papers, I am not a dictator, you know. If you can think of anything in the next twenty-four hours please let me know.' The Battlers tried desperately to think of something to stop the signing. Monica Sheehan explains[4], 'we even tried to take out a mining licence but were not successful.' Instead on 2 June 1971 they saw the leader of the Opposition, Pat Hills, who made a written appeal to Askin, stating[5], 'on behalf of the many and responsible organisations who are opposing the Government decision in this matter ... I appeal to you to take the necessary steps to have the decision for this development reversed and for the Government to take up acquisition of the land for the purpose of converting it to an Open Space Reservation'.

The Battlers delivered Hill's letter, personally, to Premier Askin at Parliament House, however, he reiterated that he could not tell his Minister what to do. Morton was not available to meet the Battlers who still hoped for a last-minute reprieve. Monica Sheehan describes their feelings[6], 'We felt a desperate sense of urgency! extremely tense, in fact "worked-up" and when his secretary said "Mr Morton is signing tomorrow" I felt broken'. This event received good coverage in the Sydney Morning Herald on 2 June 1971 in a supportive article entitled "Mums V Bulldozers". However, it made no impression on the stance of Askin or Morton and, on 3 June 1971, before leaving for a month overseas, Morton signed the document allowing the development of Kelly's Bush. It appeared, now, that all options were closed and that, if the Battlers had not possessed that "persistence against all odds" described by Mary Campbell of the National Trust, Kelly's Bush might well have been lost.

The first reaction of the Battlers, now that all else had failed, was to try to stop the bulldozers. The President, Betty James, said[7], 'we will have to stand in front of them and more importantly we had better find out which side they would be on if we take such a dramatic step.'

There are differing accounts of the next important event in the Battle for Kelly's Bush, viz. the involvement of the Trade Unions.

Roddewig claims[8], it was 'Mary Campbell, the Battlers' mentor from the National Trust, who had planted the idea in their minds at one of their organizational meetings, by explaining how Unions had saved the Great Barrier Reef from oil drilling.' I clearly recollect from my own involvement that Rodney Cavalier had explained to the Battlers that it may be possible to enlist the help of the Union movement. Jack Mundey recalls[9], 'it all just came together at the time'; while Monica Sheehan claims[10], 'it was on the advice of Bellanto, the recent unsuccessful Labor candidate, that they contacted Jack Cambourne, of the Federated Engine Drivers and Fireman's Association (NSW Branch) (FED FA), the Union that covered the bulldozer drivers, and Ray Gietzelt from the Miscellaneous Workers Union.

The executive of the Battlers immediately prepared urgent letters outlining their two-year battle to save the "Bush" for the present and succeeding generations of children and how in spite of all their efforts it was to be re-zoned as Residential. Events happened very quickly as the Labor Council would be meeting almost immediately. The letters had to be considered and debated as soon as possible and it was not known how soon Jennings would commence work on the site. Some of the more conservative Battlers were disturbed to find that the Unions had been involved without their knowledge. However, speed had been imperative -there was not time to convene a meeting- and, before long, all members ratified the executive's action.

Monica Sheehan recalls[11], both Cambourne, from the FEDFA, and Gietzelt, from the Miscellaneous Workers Union, stated that they would support them in any confrontation. As Cambourne recalled [12], 'We didn't go to the people at Kelly's Bush. They came to us.' Subsequently the letters to the two Unions were referred to the full New South Wales Trades and Labor Council with a recommendation that they pass a resolution in opposition to any development at Kelly's Bush.

Cavalier recalls[13], 'the motion to place a black ban on the "Bush" was moved by John Ducker and seconded by himself, and on the very night when the Trades and Labor Council heard the representations of the FEDFA and the other affiliated unions about Kelly's Bush, the Minister for Local Government signed the zoning change permitting the Jennings development.'

The Labor Council unanimously adopted a resolution "expressing total opposition to the development site". This did give the Battlers some breathing space, as they knew that Jennings was keen to begin building on the site almost immediately. Two weeks later a delegation from the Labor Council met with the Acting Planning Minister, Jago, to persuade him to stop the development but the State Government remained unmoved.

Then a most important event occurred: Monica Sheehan recalls[14], 'Bob Pringle, President of the Builders Labourers Federation, phoned us seeking information about Kelly's Bush and we invited him to come out and see the "Bush" for himself. He came out the next Saturday'. Betty James describes how[15], 'the situation was full of obvious ironies but the gravity of it overcame any embarrassment. We asked him how he could help. He said: "We can put a black ban on it" In a sense it was as much a new venture for the Builders Labourers Federation as it was for the Battlers'. For some of the Battlers, those from conservative Hunter's Hill backgrounds, the thought of aligning themselves with a Union run by avowed communists was very difficult. Roddewig quotes Kath Lehany's comments on the Union involvement[16], 'many members of the Hunter's Hill Trust would have nothing to do with us when the Unions became involved; they feared that the community support, that they had, would fade away if it was known that they associated with groups like the BLF.'

However, the Battlers were impressed by Pringle, who agreed to put their case to the Builders Labourers and let them know the result as soon as possible. While the Battlers waited for news of their support from the Builders Labourers they continued to pursue all other avenues, including a meeting with representatives of the Jennings Co. Kath Lehany says that she will always remember[17], 'the venue specially chosen was the home of one of the tnore conservative members of the group, an older and most respectable Hunters Hill family. We decided to only serve them tea and scones, definitely no whiskey or alcohol. She continues, describing how very patronising these gentlemen from Jennings were, implying that nice ladies should not get mixed up in such matters. The Battlers were angry that they were not taken seriously, (but remained calm and politely put their case. It was to no avail and the developers said that the building would go ahead. Then one of the great ironies of the Battle for Kelly's Bush occurred. The phone rang with the confirmation that the Battlers had been waiting for, viz. that the BLF would support them.' She goes on to describe how Betty James, after taking the call, returned to the room and just nodded to us and 'we all knew, but of course said nothing to our guests. We suddenly felt like a group of High School girls with a special secret the teacher did not know, we dared not look at each other and found it hard to keep a straight face. Then the gentlemen condescendingly decided they could waste no more time and hardly able to contain ourselves, we sold them a "Save Kelly's Bush Badge" as they left.'

In retrospect, at this stage in the Battle for Kelly's Bush, neither the Battlers, nor the Jennings Co. and certainly not the State politicians concerned, or the Local Council, had any idea just how long-term and far reaching the events of the next few weeks would be. That, soon, history would be made at Kelly's Bush with the introduction of the world's first Black, later to become, Green Ban. A new era in environmentalism in Australia was beginning.

1. Interview with Rodney Cavalier, 2 December 1995
2. Monica Sheehan, Battlers for Kelly's Bush, ML MSS 5549/3
3. Interview with Chris Dawson, 5 October 1995
4. Monica Sheehan, op. cit.
5. The Battle for Kelly's Bush, Honi Soit, 1 7 June 1971
6. Monica Sheehan. op. cit.
7. Betty James, Battlers for Kelly's Bush, ML MSS 5549/3
8. R.J. Roddewig, Green Bans, Hale & Ironmonger, Syd, 1978, 8

9. Interview with Jack Mundey, 27 September 1995
10. Monica Sheehan, op. cit.
11. Ibid.
12. Gavin Souter, Sydney Morning Herald, (article undated from Ryde Library Local Studies Centre)
13. Interview with Rodney Cavalier, op. cit.
14. Monica Sheehan, op. cit.
15. Betty James, op. cit.
16. Roddewig, op. cit, 10
17. Interview with Kath Lehany, 19 October, 1995.

Unions in the First Green Ban

Although it was the combined Unions under the Labor Council that first moved to place a black ban on Kelly's Bush, it was Jack Mundey the Communist Secretary of the Builders Labourers Federation who captured the imagination of the press and, to this day, is credited with the success and eventual popularity of the Green Ban movement. He had grown up in the beautiful Atherton Tablelands in Queensland and came to Sydney in the 1950s. He recalls[1], 'the Cullawalla Chambers was the biggest building then as there was a height limit of 150 feet (46 metres) but by the 1960s the sky was the only limit to development.' However his first priority, when elected 'Organiser' with the BLF in 1962, was to improve, for his fellow workers, the harsh conditions that had often resulted in their injury or death. Mundey explains[2], 'in one year in Sydney alone twelve dogmen had been killed in falls from buildings.'

At the Union election in 1968 Jack Mundey, Joe Owens and Bob Pringle replaced the old traditional executive of the BLF. Then, as the flow of capital increased in the Sydney building market with more jobs available and with the aggressive bargaining stance of this new energetic executive, work practices greatly improved for the Labourers. It was then that the executive had a chance to turn its attention to issues such as the environment. Mundey explained to me that[3], 'once he and his executive Pringle and Owens, had decided to align with the Battlers they had to convince the other Unionists that the well heeled upper-class people of Hunter's Hill had as much right to open space as working class people in other neighbourhoods. In fact I believed that it was little use gaining higher wages and better conditions if we lived in cities devoid of parks and denuded of trees. In the building boom in Sydney the BLF had unwittingly collaborated in the destruction of some of Sydney's most beautiful areas and buildings, replacing them with tall concrete and glass constructions. Our cities had to be for people not just for corporations to plunder and destroy.' On the other hand the Battlers had always maintained that the preservation of Kelly's Bush was for the benefit of all Sydney not just Hunter's Hill; it was a symbol and a test case. It was these points that Mundey used to convince his Unionists. He described the situation as[4], 'an alliance between the enlightened middle-class from Hunter's Hill and the enlightened working-class from the NSW Builders Labourers Federation enjoined in a common environmental struggle'.

The Battlers, encouraged by the support they had gained from the Union movement, planned to hold a public meeting at the Hunter's Hill Town Hall on the evening of 17 June 1971. The Builders Labourers had stipulated, as a condition of their intervention, that the Battlers demonstrate public interest in saving Kelly's Bush. The Battlers received support for the meeting from several local Preservation Societies, the newly formed coalition of residents' action groups (CRAG), the Australian Labor Party and the Australia Party. However, the most important support group listed on the meeting notice was the Hunter's Hill Trust. Many in the Trust were strongly opposed to support for the Battlers now that left-wing Unions were involved. Rodney Cavalier had been invited by the President, Dr Bradfield, to address the seventeen-member executive and put the case for Union involvement as the only way to save the "Bush". He recalls[5], there was a long hard debate but eventually the executive voted, by a majority of one, to support the Battlers' action in involving the Union movement.' However, there was great anxiety in the Trust over this decision. Richard Temple, long time executive member and author of the Trust's "Twenty Year History" describes the mood of the time[6], 'Some members of the Trust Committee were so concerned at the Trust allying itself with what they perceived as a 'political' (i.e. left-wing) organisation that they attempted to prevent the Trust from joining the Battlers in a meeting at the Hunter's Hill Town Hall, in June 1971, to protest against the threatened subdivision.'

Although the meeting was called at short notice the Town Hall was overflowing as more than 500 people turned out, many from outside the district.

Quoting from the Sydney Morning Herald[7], 'The meeting decided to urge the Government to reopen the matter of Kelly's Bush and to negotiate with the developers to save the entire area of 12.1 acres from development and preserve it in its natural state'. Mundey describes[8], 'The motion was unanimous and so the first of the famous Green Bans was imposed. This democratic method of imposition of Green Bans stood the Union in good stead. It clearly demonstrated that it wasn't Mundey or some other union leader arbitrarily deciding to act on the basis of his own particular judgmental values. Each ban was imposed only after a full and open public meeting had been held.'

There is no doubt that, as Roddewig describes[9], 'the use of the term green instead of black ban was a stroke of genius'. Mundey recalled how in July 1973 in an interview with Malcolm Colless, the industrial writer with the Australian[10], 'I said in future we'd be talking about green bans. The adjective green was more apt than black. It also explained our wish to extend our help to other citizens, not just unionists alone.' The terms Green, and Green Politics had been in use overseas, however the action of direct Union involvement resulting in the use of the term Green Ban began in Australia in June 1971.

The term was particularly appropriate for the first Ban as the aim was to save the Bush, whereas future Green Bans would be involved, among other things, in the preservation of historic buildings.

In a recent retrospective article in the Bulletin Mundey recalls the situation then [11], 'Green Bans heralded a new force in resident and union action. For the first time, the bluerinse set met with the blue-singletted workers of the NSW BLF to campaign for a common cause … united over a pot of tea and a plan to protect a strip of bush, the last remaining natural frontage on Sydney Harbour.' Debate continued in the community, the media and the local press. It was a good story and both sides were resolute in their opposing stances. On 25 June children from six local schools marched to Kelly's Bush where they were addressed by the local member, Peter Coleman, and the President of the Hunter's Hill Branch of the ALP, Rodney Cavalier. This event received prominent coverage in the Sydney Morning Herald. On 6 July the Herald published an article from the Hunter's Hill Trust entitled "New approach on Kelly's Bush development plan" in which the President, Dr Bradfield, criticised the Council, elected on a policy of support for the Trust, which had now backed down on the Kelly's Bush issue.

Jack Mundey recently recounted to me one of the most important developments that occurred immediately after the announcement of the ban by the BLF[12], 'A small news item appeared in the press and a spokesman for AV Jennings said that the company would not worry about the BLF's decision because he would have the buildings put up by non-union labour, if need be. This statement inflamed the situation. We called a lunchtime meeting on a half-completed, twenty-storey building site in North Sydney for which AV Jennings were contracting. The workers carried a resolution: "If one blade of grass or one tree is touched in Kelly's Bush, this half-completed building will remain for ever as a monument to Kelly's Bush". AV Jennings quickly changed their minds about the use of scab labour'. However, this statement of theirs "set the cat among the pigeons" as far as Askin and his developer friends were concerned.' They now realised that they had a real battle on their hands with more to contend with than a group of dedicated housewives. Editorials in the daily papers became critical of the BLF's stand, using the phrases 'proletarian town planners' and 'mere builders labourers'.

Burgmann wrote about the situation[13], 'At the time, the Askin Government and the mass media were totally opposed to the union activity. The Herald in fact produced five editorials in fourteen days opposing the right of the Union to undertake political action such as the Green Bans.' Mundey described how[14], 'For the first half of the 1960s, the unelected, remote and elitist State Planning Authority (SPA) had decided what was best for Sydney and New South Wales. We were not setting ourselves up as town planners, or as arbitrators of taste. However, there was a vacuum in planning procedures, there was no authority or body for people to turn to, we were just allowing ordinary people to have some say.'

The Battlers and Hunter's Hill residents, still a little uneasy about the truce in their battle to save the bush, had their defences tested when a bulldozer appeared close to Kelly's Bush on Saturday the 26 June. The bulldozer had been sent by Council to clear some building blocks which had become a fire hazard. Their telephone alarm system worked well and within a few minutes more than thirty residents surrounded the bulldozer. Quoting a report of the incident frm the Sun-Herald, Miss Kylie Tennant, the authoress who was among the protesters, said[15], 'I got the alarm and came down here with my daughter to overturn a few bulldozers. But we weren't needed this time'. My own recollections of the time were [16], 'there had always been fear of bulldozers turning up and destroying the bush before the Battlers and their supporters could intervene. This incident tested their readiness to act and, in fact, was the only time that a bulldozer ever came near Kelly's Bush.'

In early July representatives from the Jennings firm visited Sydney and put their case for development of the site to the press and the Unions. The Herald carried a long article entitled "Kelly's Bush: the case for the Company" in which A V Jennings described himself as a conservationist, discussed his building plans for the area, and ignored any reference to the Battlers or the other groups and the many residents opposed to the development. He justified his stand by stating[17], 'My feelings are that the Hunter's Hill Council represents the majority of ratepayers -they are elected democratically and they have agreed to it'. The Jennings representatives met with the Unions and a proposal was put forward -'the possibility of swapping Kelly's Bush for Government owned land.' The Unions agreed to approach the Government. However, a few days later a small piece appeared in the Sydney Morning Herald in which Morton was quoted as saying[18], 'he did not know enough details of the proposal to be able to comment.' According to Roddewig[19], 'the swap appealed to Jennings as an honourable compromise but by then the State Government was bitterly opposed to any compromise with the Battlers and their supporters.' Nothing of substance ever came of the proposal.

The next local event was a "Back to Kelly's Bush Picnic" held on 8 August 1971. Prior to this a group of young activists had set up the Kelly's Bush Citizens' Action Committee aimed at assisting the Battlers and to involve University students. It succeeded in attracting many supporters 'from Macquarie University. This new group and the Battlers sent many written invitations to political, educational, cultural and sporting bodies in NSW whose representatives and members had shown interest and support.

My own recollections of the picnic were[20], 'it was a great success, a happy lively atmosphere, as family groups such as my own mingled with the many supporters from outside the municipality.' The picnic, as well as gaining favourable publicity for the Kelly's Bush cause, encouraged other newly formed Residents Action Groups from outside Hunter's Hill. Over six hundred people were present most of whom signed a petition to the Premier protesting against the development of Kelly's Bush.

In spite of unfavourable editorials condemning the action of the Unions there were individual journalists from the daily papers who were prepared to support the new environmental movement and write in a positive way about the actions of the Battlers and the newly-formed coalition of resident action groups (CRAG) which had been formed because of widespread dissatisfaction with current town planning actions by local councils, State Government Departments and instrumentalities.

The Sun featured an article, entitled "For Progress or Posterity", which described[21], 'how successful the recent picnic was and how the Battle of Kelly's Bush is gathering momentum. The Battlers ... are strengthening their forces for the September local government elections, to support candidates who will dedicate themselves to the preservation of bushlands.' In an article in the Sydney Morning Herald, Weekend Magazine, titled "Suburbs in revolt", Margaret Jones stated[22], 'Progress Associations have always existed but the new groups are quite a different kind of phenomenon. They are producing, for the first time, a working-class middle-class coalition. They are often belligerent, even in leafy suburbs like Hunter's Hill.' It described the new Civic Design Society based at the University of New South Wales which has drawn up a register of 19 flourishing civic groups in the metropolitan area. Quoting the President of the Society, Anthony Strachan[23], 'Citizens groups are more active now because of a failure of initiative on the part of local government. We believe the groups' activities are only just beginning and from now on they will gather momentum.'

These supportive articles helped to counteract the official Government establishment view as presented, at the time, in the media. As the Council elections approached a Sydney Morning Herald journalist, Gavin Souter, produced a large feature article "Power to the People" in which he detailed the large number of Councils, particularly in the inner city, where candidates were being supported by resident-action groups.[24], 'Their platforms are concerned with environmental rather than bread and butter issues, and they are implacably opposed to development without a human face.' It concluded with a statement by the first Chairman of CRAG: 'It is vital that local government should open up its decision making ... to us development means a better quality of living. We should take a clear look at what questions of social justice are involved. Who gains, and who loses? Too often these questions are simply bulldozed out of the way.'

This article also noted that the Trust would be supporting candidates in each of Hunter's Hill's three wards in the forthcoming council elections. It was at this stage that I became personally involved in the Battle for Kelly's Bush when I decided to run for Council and give my preferences to the Trust candidate in my Ward. That candidate was Sheila Swain, a keen conservationist, Secretary of the Save the Lane Cove Valley Committee, and a well known and respected member of the local community. One of my two running mates was Rodney Cavalier who was already devoted to the task of saving Kelly's Bush. Although we were unsuccessful our preferences elected Sheila Swain who did an excellent job as an Alderman and was unrelenting in the Battle to save Kelly's Bush. She made a great contribution to Local Government and was at least twice elected Mayor of Hunters Hill. However, overall, the results of the elections in September 1971 were not encouraging as those in favour of the development had the numbers, once again, on Council. If it had not been for the Green Ban and the perseverance of the Battlers' who remained together and vigilant and kept the issue alive locally, development would have occurred, for it would be many years before the issue would be resolved.

1. Bulletin, 7 April, 1991, 57
2. Jack Munday, Green Bans and Beyond, Angus & Robertson 1982, 76
3. Interview with Jack Munday, 27 September 1995
4. Ibid
5. Interview with Rodney Cavalier, 2 December 1995
6. Richard Temple, History of Hunter's Hill Trust, 1988
7. Sydney Morning Herald, 18 June, 1971
8. Drew Hutton, ed., Green Politics in Australia, Angus & Robertson, Sydney, 1987, 108
9. Richard J Roddewigg, Green Bans, Hale & Ironmonger, Sydney, 1978 12
10. Jack Mundey, op. cit., 105
11. Bulletin, op. cit., 57
12. Interview with Jack Mundey, 27 September, 1995
13. Meredith Burgmann, Sydney Morning Herald, 18 March 1994
14. Interview with Jack Mundey, 27 September, 1995
15. Sun Herald, 27 June, 1971
16. Margaret Shaw, Author, personal recollections
17. Sydney Morning Herald, 3 July, 1971
18. Sydney Morning Herald, 8 July, 1971
19. Richard J Roddewig, op. cit.,13
20. Margaret Shaw, op. cit.
21. The Sun, 11 August, 1971.
22. Sydney Morning Herald, Weekend Magazine, 10 July, 1971,20 23 Ibid., 20
23. Sydney Morning Herald, 6 September, 1971, 6.

A SYMBOL AND A TEST CASE

SAVE KELLY'S BUSH AND YOU HELP SAVE OTHER BUSHLAND

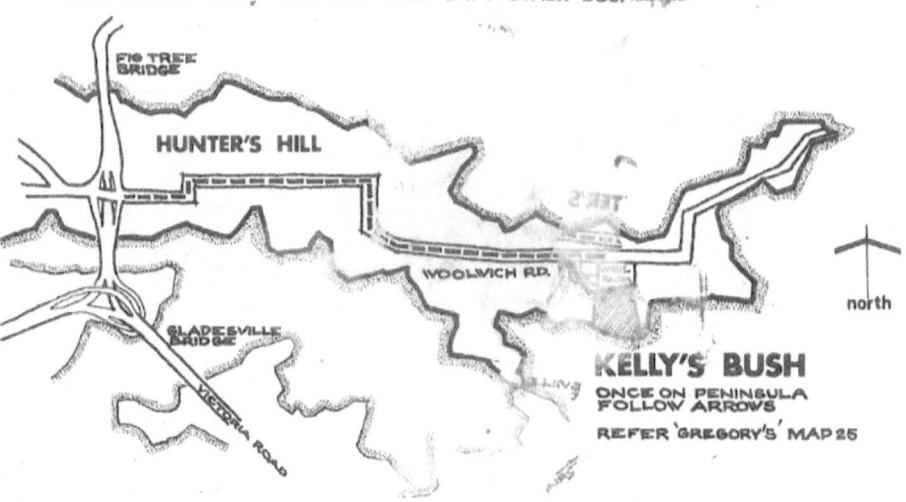

- 12 ACRES OF NATURAL BUSH
- 4 MILES RADIUS FROM G.P.O.
- USED AS RECREATION FOR PAST 80 YEARS
- VITALLY NEEDED FOR RECREATION FOR THE FUTURE

KELLY'S BUSH FOR BROWSING NOT HOUSING!

Hunters Hill High Study Group

A Green Ban at the Rocks

It was this first Green Ban that gave heart to other groups fighting against unwanted development and soon the BLF were inundated with requests for help. Before its deregulation in June 1974 they would impose forty-two Green Bans. Some would be to preserve open space or bushland others to save working class housing or historic buildings. Here I would like to discuss one of the most controversial bans which was imposed to prevent demolition of part of The Rocks to make way for the erection of new hotels, offices and high-cost residential apartments. This conflict was different from, and provides a contrast to, the situation at Kelly's Bush. It would involve working class residents and the BLF in a direct clash with the State Government and the powerful Sydney Cove Redevelopment Authority (SCRA). As the oldest residential area in Australia Blackmore describes[1], 'The Rocks in 1900 was the product of 11 decades of largely unregulated development, demolition and redevelopment superimposed on a spatial form established in the Colony's infancy ... . The area had a character all its own: in the grown-up world of the greater City of Sydney, the Rocks was an unruly adolescent.'

After an outbreak of plague in Sydney in early 1900 there were some attempts at slum clearance in The Rocks and new commercial buildings replaced the demolished houses. In the 1930s and 1950s various schemes for redevelopment were put forward which did not eventuate.

Then construction of the Harbour Bridge caused great consternation to the residents as fine old homes were demolished that stood in its path and the community suffered in terms of space and social dislocation. The construction of the Cahill expressway although causing less demolition than the bridge further isolated the Rocks from the rest of the city. However, the 1970s would bring the biggest threat to this historic area. As

Blackmore explains[2], 'these earlier intrusions, in the name of advancing technology or modernism were brutal and have had lasting effects but the next decade was to have an even more profound impact on the Rocks as Sydney entered the second long boom and the "Manhattan syndrome" saw light.'

As the Office boom of the 1960s got under way the construction of tall commercial buildings grew up around the Rocks. It was this type of development that Sir John Overall, one of the most famous urban planners in Australia, recommended when commissioned to formulate yet another plan for the area in 1966. The SCRA was set up to administer his plan and was formally constituted in January 1971. Roddewig describes[3], 'the authority was to be composed of a cross-section of Sydney political, business, and civic dignitaries; but it wound up heavily weighted towards down town business and commercial interests ... but no one thought it necessary to include any representatives of the three hundred people who lived in the East Rocks area.

The SCRA was a powerful statutory body and directly responsible to the Minister for Local Government. It immediately set about resuming any land in private ownership.

The SCRA now had a vested interest in the rapid implementation of the new scheme to recoup large profits (estimated at the time to be about $10,000,000 per annum) on the properties it was hoping to lease. It was no wonder that, with this financial incentive, the State Government instructed the SCRA to submit their plan within one year. This time limit made it impossible to consult with the residents even if the SCRA had wished to.

The Plan was unveiled in February 1971. Roddewig describes[4]; 'The land use, height and density scheme, as announced, envisioned two-thirds of the area being cleared and rebuilt as commercial office space. Almost five million square feet of net useable office and retail space was proposed, more than double the amount proposed by Sir John Overall'. As was to be expected, the press had nothing but praise for the plan whereas it generated a strong reaction from the residents.

On disclosure of the plan, The Rocks residents, under the leadership of Nita McCrae, formed a Resident Action Group (RAG). McCrae's family had lived in the Rocks for four generations as Mundey describes, 'Nita McCrae quickly developed into an ideal leader. She knew everyone in the area

The residents had been concerned for some time about their homes and the lack of maintenance now that SCRA had become their landlord replacing the Maritime Services Board. However, it was not until the day the plans were made public that they realised what the new development would mean for them. Like some of the strange coincidences in the Kelly's Bush Battle, the Residents had their first meeting on the day that the SCRA had scheduled its big VIP press conference to unveil the development. Hardman describes their reaction to the plan[6], 'The plan enraged local residents. There was no provision for their future accommodation either within or without the redevelopment.' It provided only for the preservation of a token number of historical buildings which would be overshadowed by huge high-rise constructions.

The Residents began, like the Battlers, circulating petitions and writing to the State government but to no avail. Battler Chris Dawson recalled, saying[7], 'in November 1971 Nita McCrae discussed with me the possibility of seeking help from the BLF and I strongly advised her to contact them immediately'. As with Kelly's Bush the BLF advised that residents hold a meeting, -over 1000 attended- and the Green Ban, this time on a working-class, inner-city neighbourhood, was on.

In January the first serious confrontation occurred between the residents and some non-BLF demolition workers. This action led to the Bulldozer operators' Union, the FEDFA, and a number of other Unions joining the Rocks Green Ban and declaring support for the residents.

For Askin the Rocks Green Ban was a far more serious problem than Kelly's Bush and brought the BLF and residents in direct conflict with the Government. Newspaper editorials, such as this scathing one in the Sydney Morning Herald, reflected the Governments stance[8]; 'The BLF's new-found concern for moral issues is touching. Hitherto, it has been much known for encouraging or condoning violence by its members no doubt it wishes to rid itself of that malodorous reputation, and what better way to do so than by jumping on the environmental bandwagon ... grandiose posturing about moral issues ... cynical opportunism ... there is absolutely no case for a union black ban, which is very likely to discourage major investors, knock the bottom out of a generally desirable scheme and reduce employment opportunities in the industry.' It was clear, at this time, that the Herald was right behind the Government in their opposition to this Green Ban.

It is, then, not surprising that one of the biggest confrontations in the history of Green Bans took place at the Rocks in October 1973. Resident Groups from outside the area and Unionists joined with the Rocks Residents to prevent the demolition, by scab labour, of some old buildings in Playfair Street, to make way for the construction of a five storey block of home units. The incident received wide coverage in the media including a large leading article in the Sydney Morning Herald. It described how[9], 'Police Embroiled at The Rocks arrested seventy-seven protesters', the article concluded with a statement by the Leader of the Opposition, Pat Hills which echoed the sentiments of many people at that time[10], 'the Government had caused a breakdown in respect for law and order and forced citizens to go elsewhere to preserve the environment and their rights. Self-respecting conservative people have turned to communist trade-union leaders like Jack Mundey to protect them from councils, from the State Planning Authority and even decisions by the Minister for Local Government.'

There were many graphic scenes on television and in newspapers picturing Jack Mundey and others being carried from the site by police. In a lengthy article by Evan Whitton in the National Times entitled "The Greenies' hero is fighting for survival -and so, some say, is Sydney" Mundey explained[11], 'My belief is that Askin wants to provoke a bloody clash as election ammunition and that Colonel Magee (director of the SCRA) deliberately provoked an incident.' In the same article Battler Lehany agreed that[12], 'the events at the Rocks were the first shots in what is to be a law and order election. Many of my friends feel that if the Green Bans go, for whatever reason, it will be the end of Sydney.' There was a danger at this time in the Green Ban movement that the goodwill built up with the establishment greenies and the BLF would collapse if violence continued.

Mundey was aware of this problem as Whitton explains[13], 'he sought an agreement from the Premier and Magee that they would attend a meeting to be chaired by Tom Uren, the new Federal Minister for Urban and Regional Development, and that non-union labour was to be removed from The Rocks.' At a rally of Unionists and residents the following day he cautioned them against being provoked into "violent confrontation with the police". Unfortunately, this use of non-union labour at the Rocks did lead to strike action and even after a return to work the Master Builders Association threatened a lock out until all Green Bans were lifted. An article in the Financial Review sums up the situation[14], 'Mr Uren said the dispute between the building unions and the Master Builders Association is basically a question of green bans. It is apparent that the New South Wales Government is seeking to destroy the entire green bans process overnight without replacing it by any rational process'

The Green Ban on the Rocks was probably the one that most angered Premier Askin, the one he most wanted to smash. There was a great deal of capital tied up both by Government and development companies. The SCRA, also desperate to break the ban, placed advertisements in the Sydney Morning Herald, e.g.[15], 'The Red Ban On The Rocks: This is not a green ban in the Rocks -it is a RED ban placed by the union which places itself above the law. It has nothing to do with conservation'.

These advertisements and the editorials in the Sydney Morning Herald conveniently ignored the fact that it was the residents that asked for the bans as they had been completely ignored by the SCRA. There were several further attempts to smash the Green Ban by using scab labour, however it remained in place. A new group calling itself The Rocks Peoples' Plan

Committee, under the chairmanship of the architect Neville Gruzman, was formed. Roddewig describes [16],

'they opted for maintenance of the Rocks as an integrated residential and historic area, separated from the functions of the central business district. Its major recommendations formed the basis on which the Rocks RAG would lift the green bans and allow redevelopment to proceed.

With the change to a Labor Government in the Federal sphere, the Department of Urban and Regional Development was established in 1973. As this gradually influenced public opinion about unrestrained development even the most conservative State Government was now forced to respond. By the mid 1970s no major development had commenced at the Rocks and even the SCRA agreed that future planning should place greater importance upon cultural, social and historical values and less upon the possible economic return that was implicit in the 1970 plan. Unlike the Kelly's Bush situation, the Rocks Green Ban involved more fundamental issues, in that it presented a challenge to the very nature of Australian urban planning, as it took on the powerful statutory body the SCRA. However, like Kelly's Bush, it allowed the public voice to be heard as it demonstrated wide disillusionment with the political processes of the time. As the Green Ban saved Kelly's Bush, not just for the residents of Hunter's Hill but for all Sydney to enjoy, so The Green Ban on the Rocks not only retained it as a viable place for the residents but also enabled it to retain its unique character as a lovely place to visit both for Australians and for tourists from overseas.

1. Kate Blackmore, Design of Sydney, ed. G P Webber, Law Book Co., Sydney, 1988,121
2. Ibid.,128
3. Richard J Roddewig, Green Bans, Hale & Ironmonger, Sydney, 1978, 18
4. Ibid., 20
5. Jack Mundey, Green Bans and Beyond, Angus & Robertson, 1982, 89
6. M Hardman & P. Manning, Green Bans, Australian Conservation Foundation, Melbourne, 1975
7. Interview with Chris Dawson, 5 October, I 995

8. Sydney Morning Herald, 11 August, 1972
9. Sydney Morning Herald, 25 October, 1973
10. 10 Ibid.
11. Evan Whitton, The National Times, 29 Oct-3 Nov, 1973, 6 12 Ibid., 6
12. Ibid., 6
13. Financial Review, 6 November, 1973
14. Sydney Morning Herald, 27 October, 1973
15. Richard Roddewig, op. cit., 25.

RED FACES—NEAR RIOT AT KELLYS BUSH

A council order to clear two building lots which had become fire hazards almost caused a riot at Hunters Hill yesterday morning.

More than 30 residents flocked to Kelly's Bush when a bulldozer appeared shortly after 7 am.

A controversy has raged for more than 12 months between the residents, who want the 61 acres of harbourside scrub preserved, and a development company which plans to subdivide it into 25 homesites.

The residents thought yesterday's bulldozer was the first move by the developers to clear the area.

After abusing the driver of the machine, Mr Laurie Hodge, for 15 minutes, the residents discovered he had arrived to clear the two building blocks that adjoin Kelly's Bush.

"It looked pretty nasty for a while," Mr Hodge said later.

Lie down

"I didn't know if I should just drive through the people or call the police.

"There were kids with banners all around my bulldozer and the adults were abusing me.

"Finally, the bloke who hired me turned up and sorted it all out."

By yesterday afternoon, Mr Hodge had cleared most of the scrub from building blocks.

The president of the battlers for Kelly's Bush, Mrs Elizabeth James, said the locals were prepared to lie down in front of any tractors or bulldozers that came to clear the reserve.

"Today it was a false alarm but it shows we are ready for action," she said.

"One woman came here today with some rope to tie herself to a tree."

Miss Kylie Tennant, the authoress, who was among the protestors said: "I put the alarm and came down here with my daughter to overturn a few bulldozers.

"But we weren't needed this time."

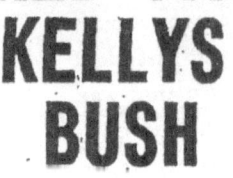
Some who turn Kelly's) a buldoz false ala

The bulldozer that started the false alarm.

Press report of the "bulldozer incident" at Kelly's Bush

Other Important Green Bans

The Ban on the Rocks attracted so much publicity that the movement quickened apace and from the first Green Ban at Kelly's Bush in June 1971 to the end of the period in March 1975, 42 Green Bans were imposed. They fell into many different categories and were only used when all else had failed. Jack Mundey always maintained the proponents had to demonstrate they had strong support in their community. Two of the most controversial and publicised Green Bans were Victoria Street,. at Kings Cross, and Woolloomooloo. The former, became notorious because of the treatment of the squatters who tried to stay on in the terrace houses to prevent their demolition for replacement by 45 storey tower blocks. Juanita Neilsen, who spoke out about the development in her newspaper Now, disappeared during the time of the ban and was presumed murdered. Finally after the loss of millions of dollars, the developer agreed to scale down the construction and much of the streetscape was retained.

By the time the Green Ban on Woolloomooloo was declared many families had been evicted by the developer as he prepared to erect high rise housing. Under the capable leadership of the Parish Priest, Father Campion, a Resident Action Group was formed and a Green Ban was soon in place. This held firm until 1975, as a news item from the Sydney· Morning Herald describes 'last week a Builders Labourers Federation Green Ban, which had been in force for more than three years, was lifted from the area as a prelude to a Federal/State agreement'. With Commonwealth money, a sensitive construction of medium density Housing Commission development took place.

Two other well-known Green Bans involved saving Centennial Park from becoming a sports stadium and opposing the construction of an Opera House car park that involved the destruction of old Moreton Bay

Fig trees. In the case of Centennial Park, Mundey describes how he had support from such unlikely allies as Patrick White, Cardinal Gilroy and entrepreneur Harry M Miller. On Australia Day in 1974 Patrick White named Jack Mundey as one of three Australians who deserved to be standing in his place to receive the award of Australian of the Year. He described Mundey as 'the first citizen of Australia's increasingly benighted, shark infested city to effectively succeed in calling the bluff of those who had begun tearing us to bits, ostensibly in the name of progress, but in fact for their own aggrandisement, with little regard for human needs.'

1. Sydney Morning Herald, 20 June, 1975
2. The Australian, 26 January, 1974.

A Split in the BLF

By 1974, the developers had many projects tied up by Green Bans. Therefore it was not surprising that they should try, through the Master Builders Association, to bring pressure on the unions. As Mundey stood firm on his conservation principles they would seek to do this through the Federal Secretary, Norm Gallagher. Boyd describes differences between Mundey's attitude and that of the Federal Council of the Building Construction Workers' Federation [1]; 'The Federal Council calls for a balanced campaign on conservation issues but Jack Mundey says his NSW Branch will stand firm on every single Green Ban we have and that his members have no intention of becoming puppets of developers. Then a resolution warns that any branch of the union who fails to carry its decisions could suffer intervention - a take over of the Branch by Federal officials.' In June 1974 the Master Builders Association of New South Wales, acting through the Australian Industrial Court, was finally successful in having the entire Australian BLF deregistered. Initially Gallagher had fought against the deregistration but, after it had occurred, he sought to reregister the union without the NSW Branch.

Mundey and his supporters continued to run their old NSW Branch as before but were eventually outmanoeuvred by Gallagher as employers would not accept any workers unless they were members of the new Federal Branch. In March 1975 Mundey tried unsuccessfully to get back with his supporters into the Federal body and called for fresh elections. This was not acceptable to the Federal Council and in April 1975 Mundey and twenty-three colleagues were expelled.

Roddewig explains[2], 'Although charges of graft and corruption and the issue of who was the bigger capitalist lackey played a major role in the Gallagher Mundey battle, "jobs or green bans" was the underlying issue.' The scope of Green Ban activities would now be reduced as the new leadership lacked the vision of Mundey, Pringle and Owens. However, by 1975 there was a new awareness in the community towards environmental issues and a great deal of credit for this goes to the BLF under the old leadership.

1. Brian Boyd, Inside the B.L.F., Ocean Press, Melbourne, 1991, 10
2. Richard J Roddewig, Green Bans, Hale & Ironmonger, Sydney, 1978, 106.

Victory for the Battlers

By 1975, though many of the Green Bans had been successful in producing a satisfactory settlement, the Kelly's Bush issue remained outstanding. It surfaced again in the National Times of March 1975 in an article that dealt with the Environmental Impact Study on Kelly's Bush completed by Jennings Industries in May 1974. The study had only just become available to Hunter's Hill Trust and the Battlers. The Trust had assumed that the study must have been weak or it would have been released earlier, in fact this was the case. However, it was now released to the Planning and Environment Council (the old SPA) who in turn sent a copy to the unions. The SPA had long been an advocate of development at Kelly's Bush. Both the Battlers and the Unions knew that the resolution of the issue was overdue but agreed that there must be complete preservation of the Bush. The Secretary of the Battlers, Kath Lehany, says[1], 'the Battlers are alive and well though we get the feeling that sometimes that someone is just waiting for us to fall asleep.'

Kelly's Bush again made news in the local and Sydney daily press at the end of 1976 and early '77. In December the much awaited Hunter's Hill Town Plan was discussed in Council and the version it would submit to the State Government was passed at an open meeting. However, Kelly's Bush still remained a problem. When the plan was first placed on public exhibition in 1973 Lot 3 of Kelly's Bush was zoned residential [2(2a)]. There were eight objections lodged including those from the Battlers and the Hunters Hill Trust. The Council had engaged Commissioner Dale, a retired town planner, to examine these and any other objections to the town plan. On the issue of Kelly's Bush he upheld the objections to the residential zoning claiming[2], 'I am of the opinion that it should be preserved for posterity and recommend the area be reserved as "County

Open Space". As part of the overall plan to preserve the existing character of Hunter's Hill the area should all be open space'. The late Alderman, Moira Baird, who gave constant support to the Battlers in Council, in moving the motion of support for Commissioner Dale's recommendation, suggested that as there is in State Parliament a new Government, which claims to be more sympathetic to the environment, -we should give them an opportunity to purchase or swap land for it -let us test their sincerity. The Mayor, Alderman Farrant, who had always taken an anti-Kelly's Bush stance and still had the numbers on Council opposed the motion.

This attitude by Council provoked a flurry of articles like one from the environment writer, Joseph Glascott, in the Sydney Morning Herald asking[3], 'Who will pay up for Kelly's Bush?'.

There was an angry response from Premier Wran, as articles in the Sydney Morning Herald, The Sun and the local Weekly Times, quoted him as saying[4], 'I am staggered that the Council could be so disdainful of public opinion, its lack of sensitivity is a strong argument for amalgamation'.

Once again the opposing players were lining up in the Battle for Kelly's Bush. They were Mayor Farrant, Alderman Merrington (a member of Council for 15 years), who had always favoured development, and other Aldermen who had continued to vote with them for development at Kelly's Bush. They continued to oppose the Battlers and the other community groups such as the Trust. They would not have wanted to approach the new Wran Government for assistance to buy the Bush.

Council's retention of the residential zoning also brought Jennings back to Kelly's Bush to meet with the Battlers and again float the ideas either to exchange it for another piece of land or to sell the land at cost $450,000. But, they claimed, no authority wants to buy it.

In January 1977 Premier Wran offered to pay half the cost of the land if the Council would meet the other half. He also stated that the Government would ensure that no development would occur at Kelly's Bush. However, Council claimed it could not afford to pay the other half and in February 1977 The National Trust sponsored an appeal for $100,000 to help Council acquire the land.

A further complication arose with the discovery of radioactive material in the old smelting works now part of the proposed foreshore reserve. Quoting a report in the Weekly Times of 2 March 1975, 'The Health Commission is still investigating other deposits of slag in the area and says that while the level of radiation is not dangerous, the situation is undesirable and is being treated seriously.' This brought Kelly's Bush onto the front pages of the evening papers but did nothing to solve the real problems. Cavalier claimed that it was[6] ' "a media beat-up" as further tests revealed there was no real danger to residents or contamination of Kelly's Bush'. The publicity was helpful to those against development, by making the land less desirable for residential purposes and as a delaying tactic until the State Government was able to purchase the land.

There was a long uneasy pause and then the welcome announcement by Neville Wran on 4th September 1983 that Kelly's Bush would be set aside for full public access on a permanent basis. At last the long Battle was over and Kelly's Bush had been saved for future generations. After thirteen long years the thirteen Battlers had won against overwhelming odds. There is no doubt that, once Rodney Cavalier became the local Member, he was better able to lobby the State Government to purchase the land. Battler Monica Sheehan recognised his contribution: quoting her letter dated 22 September 1987, 'The Battlers worked hard in early days but not a lot we could do in the later years you not only had the power, but also the dedication to pursue the objective, that finally won the "Battle of the Bush" Our eternal gratitude Rod and also to the Labor Party for keeping its promise'.

Cavalier, in turn, explained to me that[8], 'the Battlers role was vitally important because without them there would have been no opposition. They were crucial. to Kelly's Bush; it would not have been saved without them.' On the other hand if the Battlers had not, at the crucial moment, been supported in their struggle by the Unions, particularly the FEDFA and the BLF, the "Bush" would have gone to the developers. Jack Mundey,

Joe Owens and Bob Pringle always gave generous support to the Battlers. Probably because of their middle-class background, the Battlers felt that they needed guidance in their new radical venture. Mundey always referred to the Battlers as his[9] 'Middle-class morning-tea Matrons.'

1. Tony Maiden, National Times, March, 3-8, 1977
2. Hunters Hill Trust Journal, Vol 5, No 3, December 1976
3. Joseph Glascott Sydney Morning Herald, 30 December, 1976,24.
4. Sydney Morning Herald, 29 December, 1976, 2
5. Weekly Times, 2 March, 1977
6. Interview with Rodney Cavalier, 2 December, 1995
7. Monica Sheehan, Battlers for Kelly's Bush, ML MSS 5549/3
8. Rodney Cavalier, op. cit.
9. Richard J Roddewig, Green Bans, Hale & ironmonger, 1978, 11

Conclusion

In the relatively short period of history covered in this study of Kelly's Bush a revolution in environmental thinking has taken place. Australia had been slow to appreciate the significance of her colonial heritage and to take steps to preserve it. One of the most important steps in the battle to change Australian attitudes began with the world's first Green Ban at Kelly's Bush. As the Green-Ban movement grew in the early 1970s it generated widespread and intense controversy, as those involved were accused by the daily press, and politicians of being disruptive and anarchic. However, this controversy brought the issues involved, either the retention of open space, or the preservation of historic buildings, to the attention of the public in a manner that bodies such as The National Trust and the Australian Conservation Foundation had not found possible before.

At the time of the first Green Ban on Kelly's Bush, in June 1971, there was a widespread dissatisfaction with current town-planning actions by local Councils, State Government Departments and instrumentalities. There were no participatory avenues for people to contribute or appeal to, and it was this vacuum that the Builders Labourers Federation filled until adequate legislation arrived. The real importance of the Green-Ban movement of the early 1970s is that it brought the environment into the political arena at the same time forging new social alliances. It was a complex phenomenon, coinciding with a period of unrest in Society as it crossed traditional social, institution and political lines. In the case of Kelly's Bush it aligned the normally conservative upper-middle class, Battlers with the blue- collar workers (Unions). It was this coalition of classes that made the new movement such a formidable one. Jack Mundey describes the situation at the time as follows[1], 'intelligent action around an issue does tap a real feeling among people, even though it might be dormant. A type of action which punches through mass apathy and captures people's imagination, as it were, brings in mass support and attracts all sorts of people, for example, Patrick White.'

The election of a Labor Government in 1972 and the establishment of a Department of Urban and Regional Planning under the capable Ministry of Tom Uren put the environment on the Commonwealth agenda, particularly in the sphere of inner city urban renewal. In May 1976 Neville Wran brought Labor to power in New South Wales, introduced the Land and Environment Court and strengthened legislation to preserve our Heritage Buildings. These measures, in spite of their shortcomings, were important milestones on the way to achieving the more enlightened community attitudes to the environment that exist today.

In spite of some good legislation over the years since the Green Bans, there is still a need for individuals to take responsibility and be ever watchful in their own environment in their suburb or street. The form of the city of Sydney today would be a great deal different if it had not been for the efforts of Jack Mundey, the Builders Labourers' Federation and the residents' action groups, who together fought long, hard battles against the developers. No where is this fight better illustrated than by the Battlers who refused to admit defeat even when the going was very rough. Battler Chris Dawson explained how they always kept in mind the words of the late Kylie Tennant who was one of their keen supporters these words spoken at one of the early meetings[2]: 'Kelly's Bush is a symbol of our lost land. Take away Kelly's Bush and you take away one more assurance that in man is left a possibility for the future. The unborn Australian will ask for his birthright and be handed a piece of concrete. If Kelly's Bush and all the other harmless and beautiful places go, you have done something really sinister. The only people who have a right to be proud are those who exerted their utmost efforts to see that it should remain.'

I would like to conclude with a tribute from Richard Temple, a long time resident of Hunter's Hill and a founding member of the Hunter's Hill Trust. He writes about Kelly's Bush in the "Twenty Years of History of the

Hunter's Hill Trust[3] : 'Preserving Kelly's Bush in its entirety was not only notable for keeping one of the few remaining large parcels of harbourside bushland intact but because it will stand as an example to those involved in the conservation and preservation movement that tenacity of purpose and a determination to continue the fight for that which is worthy of preservation can succeed, even against seemingly impossible odds'.

1. Australian Left Review, December, 1973.
2. Battlers for Kelly's Bush, ML MSS, 5549/3
3. Richard Temple, Twenty Years of History of the Hunters Hill Trust, 1988.

This plaque is dedicated to the thirteen local women who battled for thirteen years to prevent Kelly's Bush from development. They became known as the Battlers for Kelly's Bush.

With the help of the Union movement and the Builders Labourers Federation in particular, Kelly's Bush became the site of the world's first Green Ban in 1971, and was saved for posterity. It is now listed on the Environmental Heritage Schedule of Hunter's Hill Council and on the NSW State Heritage Register.

THE BATTLERS FOR KELLY'S BUSH

Betty James – President
Kath Lehany – Secretary
Monica Sheehan – Assistant Secretary
Jo Bell
Kathleen Chubb
Joan Croll
Christena Dawson
Mary Farrell
Marjorie Fitzgerald
Miriam Hamilton
Trude Kallir
Margaret Stobo
Judith Taplin

This plaque also recognises the **Friends of Kelly's Bush** who regenerate and care for the bush. The group was started in 1995 by Peta Hinton and Connie Ewald.

Bibliography

Primary Sources :
Sydney, Mitchell Library, ML MSS 5549/3,
"Battlers for Kelly's Bush"
3 Boxes of records 1969 - 1985 compiled by Kath Lehany. Documents consulted included general correspondence, papers, brochures, minute book, newspapers, cuttings and printed material. "Monica Sheehan's - Re-action and thoughts on Union involvement in "Kelly's Bush".

Ryde Library & Information Services Local Studies Collection.

Hunters Hill Council, Minutes of ordinary meetings for the years 1968,69,70,71.

Access to personal papers and press cuttings relating to their role as Battlers, Chris Dawson, Treasurer and Trude Kallir Executive Committee Member.

Oral Sources :
Rodney Cavalier, Peter Coleman, Jack Mundey:
Battlers Chris Dawson, Trude Kallir and Kath Lehany: Sheila Swain, former Mayor of Hunters Hill
Alice Oppen, past President of Hunters Hill Trust.

Printed Primary Sources

Newspapers, Periodicals and other Journals:
- The Australian
- Daily Mirror
- The Sun
- The National Times
- Current Affairs Bulletin
- Sydney Morning Herald
- Sunday Mirror
- The Bulletin
- Australian Left Review
- Hunters Hill Trust Journals
- Arena (Macquarie University)
- Honi Soit (Sydney University)
- Wallumetta Journal of RHHFFPS
- Weekly Times (Local paper Gladesville/Hunters Hill) Kelly's Bush History sheet, (Hunters Hill Council)
- Newsletters from the Hunters Hill Branch of the ALP.

Secondary Sources

Alomes, Stephen, *A Nation at Last?*,
Angus & Robertson, Sydney, 1988

Bolton, Geoffrey, *The Oxford History of Australia, Vol. 5 The Middle Way 1942-1988*

Bolton, Geoffrey, *Spoils and Spoilers*,
Allen & Unwin, Sydney, 1992

Boyd, Brian, *Inside the BLF*,
Ocean Press, Melbourne, 1991, page 69

Burgmann, Verity & Lee, Jenny, eds., *Staining the Wattle*,
McPhee & Gribble, Penguin, Victoria, 1988

Flower, Cedric, *Illustrated History of N.S.W.*,
Rigby, 1981

Grimshaw, Patricia, *Creating a Nation*,
McPhee Gribble, Victoria, 1994

Hagen, Jim & Turner, Ken.,
A History of the Labour Party of N.S.W. 1891-1991,
Longman Cheshire, Melbourne, 1991

Halligan, John & Paris, Chris, *Australian Urban Politics*,
Longman Cheshire, Melbourne, 1984

Hardman, Marion & Manning, Peter, *Green Bans*,
Australian Conservation Foundation, Melbourne, n.d.

Hickie, David, *The Prince and the Premier*,
Angus Robertson, Sydney, 1985

Hutton, Drew, ed., *Green Politics in Australia*,
Angus Robertson, Sydney, 1987

Mundey, Jack, *Green Bans and Beyond*,
Angus Robertson, Sydney, 1981

Molony, John, *The Penguin History of Australia*,
Penguin Books, Victoria, 1988

Roddewig, Richard, J, *Green Bans*,
Hale & Ironmonger, Sydney, 1988

Summers, Anne et.al.
The Little Green Book the Facts on Green Bans,
Tomato Press, Sydney, 1974

Temple, Richard, *Twenty Year History of the Hunters Hill Trust* 1988

Thomas, Pete, *Taming the Concrete Jungle*, Quality Press, Sydney, 1973

Webber, G.P., ed., *The Design of Sydney*, Law Book Co. Ltd., Sydney, 1988.

www.ingramcontent.com/pod-product-compliance
Lightning Source LLC
Chambersburg PA
CBHW020330010526
44107CB00054B/2050